A **TRUE** BOOK™

NATURAL DISASTER!

All About Earthquakes

Discovering How Earth Moves and Shakes

Libby Romero

Children's Press®
An imprint of Scholastic Inc.

Content Consultant
Dr. Kristen Rasmussen
Assistant Professor
Department of Atmospheric Science
Colorado State University

Library of Congress Cataloging-in-Publication Data
Names: Romero, Libby, author.
Title: All about earthquakes / by Libby Romero.
Description: First edition. | New York : Children's Press, an imprint of Scholastic Inc., 2021. | Series: A true book: natural disaster! | Includes bibliographical references and index. | Audience: Ages 8–10. | Audience: Grades 4–6. | Summary: "This book shows readers the awesome power of earthquakes"—Provided by publisher.
Identifiers: LCCN 2021003966 (print) | LCCN 2021003967 (ebook) | ISBN 9781338769463 (library binding) | ISBN 9781338769517 (paperback) | ISBN 9781338769524 (ebook)
Subjects: LCSH: Earthquakes—Juvenile literature. | Earthquakes—History—Juvenile literature. | Seismology—Juvenile literature.
Classification: LCC QE534.3 .R66 2021 (print) | LCC QE534.3 (ebook) | DDC 551.22—dc23
LC record available at https://lccn.loc.gov/2021003966
LC ebook record available at https://lccn.loc.gov/2021003967

10 9 8 7 6 5 4 3 2 1   22 23 24 25 26

Printed in the U.S.A. 113
First edition, 2022

Series produced by Priyanka Lamichhane
Book design by Kathleen Petelinsek
Illustrations on pages 42–43 by Gary LaCoste

Front cover: Background: A road is destroyed after an earthquake; top: Earthquakes under the ocean can cause tsunamis like this one; top right: A search and rescue dog searches for people in the rubble after an earthquake; bottom: People sit outdoors to stay safe from aftershocks after an earthquake in Nepal in 2015.

Back cover: Rubble covers a street after an earthquake in Italy in 2016.

Find the Truth!

Everything you are about to read is true *except* for one of the sentences on this page.

Which one is **TRUE**?

T or F   Earthquakes happen along cracks in Earth's surface.

T or F   Most earthquakes happen in an area surrounding the Atlantic Ocean.

Find the answers in this book.

What's in This Book?

The **BIG** Truth

Images from the spacecraft Messenger show cliff-like landforms on planet Mercury.

Do Earthquakes Only Happen on Earth?

A tsunami flooded this Japanese town after a powerful earthquake in 2011.

3 Famous Earthquakes

When and where have some of the most powerful earthquakes occurred?

4 Earthquake Safety

How can people stay safe during an earthquake?

Ancient Chinese scientist Zhang Heng studied earthquakes.

中國人民郵政 8 分
張衡(公元78-139)天文學家,發明
渾天儀和地動儀
(125)1955

5

Shake, Rattle, and Roll

At 5:12 a.m. on April 18, 1906, a massive **earthquake** struck the San Francisco Bay Area in central California in the United States. Dressed in their pajamas, people ran from their homes. All around them, houses and **buildings crumbled**. The **streets rippled** like waves on the ocean.

The San Francisco earthquake is considered one of the worst natural disasters in United States history.

The earthquake—a sudden, **violent shaking** of the earth—lasted less than a minute. Then, the gas lines broke, starting **fires** throughout the city. The water lines broke, too, making it hard to fight the flames. The blazes burned for three days, leaving the city in ruins. Today, we know a lot more about earthquakes than we did then, including how they happen and how to stay safe. Read on to learn more.

Fires burned nearly 500 city blocks after the San Francisco earthquake.

The Alaska Earthquake Center detects an earthquake about every 15 minutes in the state.

A strong earthquake that struck Ecuador in 2016 caused a huge crack in this road.

Understanding Earthquakes

Earth may look like a rock-solid planet, but beneath the surface, it is very active. In fact, millions of earthquakes happen every year. Most are so small that people can't feel them. But others can cause massive damage. To understand how and why earthquakes occur, we have to understand Earth's structure.

Earth's Structure

Earth is a rocky planet made up of layers. The deepest layer is the solid inner core. Next comes the liquid outer core. The third layer is the mantle, which is divided into upper and lower sections. Earth's top layer, where we live, is the crust. The crust and top of the mantle form a shell around Earth. Over time, that shell broke into pieces called **tectonic plates**. The edges where tectonic plates meet are called **tectonic plate boundaries**.

Earth's Structure

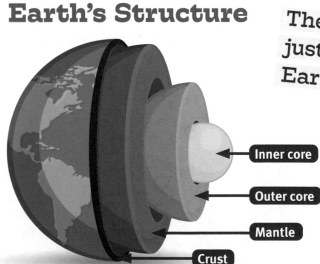

Inner core

Outer core

Mantle

Crust

The crust makes up just one percent of Earth's **mass**.

Over millions of years, rock in the mantle melts, rises toward the surface, cools, sinks, and melts again. This happens over and over.

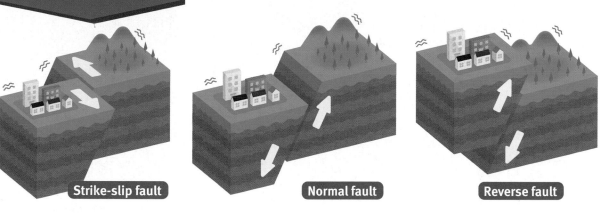

The San Andreas Fault in California is a strike-slip fault along a tectonic plate boundary.

Fault Types

Strike-slip fault

Normal fault

Reverse fault

Faults

A **fault** is a crack between two blocks of rock. All tectonic plate boundaries are faults, and most earthquakes occur along these boundaries. Earthquakes also occur along fault lines found within tectonic plates. There are different kinds of faults. At strike-slip faults, blocks of rock slide past each other. At normal faults, blocks move away from each other and one side slides down. At reverse faults, blocks of rock push against each other. One side rises and the other side slides underneath.

Epicenter: the point on the surface directly above the focus

Plates: giant moving pieces of Earth's crust and the very top of the mantle

Earthquakes happen when Earth's tectonic plates move.

Seismic waves: waves that carry energy released by an earthquake

Focus: the point deep in Earth where the earthquake started

Fault: a crack between two plates or blocks of rock along which movement occurs

When an Earthquake Strikes

The edges of tectonic plates are rough. Sometimes, one of these rough edges can get stuck along a fault, or crack, while the rest of the tectonic plate keeps moving. When enough pressure builds, a block breaks off deep inside Earth's crust. Some of the energy created by the break travels up to a point on Earth's surface, called the **epicenter**. The ground shakes as **seismic waves** carry the energy out in all directions.

Seismic Waves

There are different types of seismic waves. Body waves travel through the inside of Earth. P-waves, or primary waves, are body waves that move together and apart as they race forward. S-waves, or secondary waves, shake the ground up and down and sideways. Once body waves reach Earth's surface, some of their energy is converted to surface waves. Surface waves can shake Earth's surface from side to side or cause it to move like waves on the ocean.

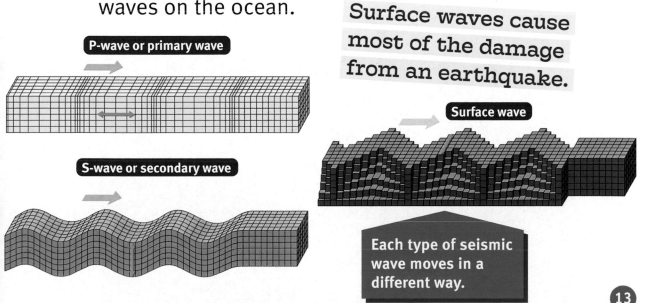

P-wave or primary wave

S-wave or secondary wave

Surface waves cause most of the damage from an earthquake.

Surface wave

Each type of seismic wave moves in a different way.

Foreshocks, Aftershocks, and Swarms

An earthquake isn't usually a one-time event. Foreshocks are smaller earthquakes that often shake the ground before a big earthquake, or mainshock, occurs. Aftershocks are a series of earthquakes that happen after a mainshock. Aftershocks may occur for days, weeks, or even years after. Sometimes a bunch of small earthquakes happen when there is no mainshock. This is called a swarm.

Many aftershocks followed a 2015 earthquake in Nepal. People stayed away from buildings to keep safe.

Tsunamis

About 90 percent of all earthquakes happen in the Ring of Fire, a path around the Pacific Ocean where many tectonic plates meet and where there are many volcanoes. A lot of the earthquakes that occur here happen underwater. Underwater earthquakes are especially dangerous. They can trigger destructive waves called **tsunamis** that zip across the ocean. When they reach land, the waves slow down and pile up into large waves. The series of waves that wash on shore can be more than 100 feet (30 meters) tall.

Ring of Fire

Tsunamis can travel up to 500 miles per hour (805 kph).

Tsunamis don't start as huge waves. The waves build as they reach land. In this photo, a boat tries to stay afloat as a tsunami hits the city of Miyako, Japan.

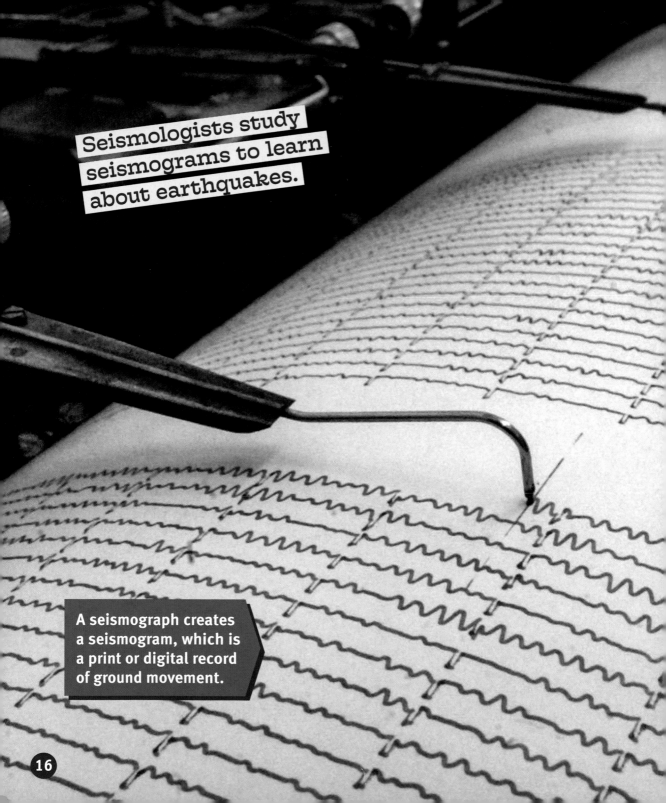

Seismologists study seismograms to learn about earthquakes.

A seismograph creates a seismogram, which is a print or digital record of ground movement.

Studying Earthquakes

About 2,000 years ago, Chinese scientist Zhang Heng invented the first seismoscope. His device could detect when earthquakes happened. If the ground shook even a little bit, a ball dropped from a dragon's head into the open mouth of a bronze frog sitting below. Today, **seismologists** use **seismographs**. These instruments record ground movement during an earthquake.

A model of Zhang Heng's seismoscope

Amatrice, Italy, before the quake

Amatrice, Italy, after the quake

Amatrice, Italy, was near the epicenter of an earthquake in 2016. Half of the town was destroyed.

Finding the Epicenter

Seismologists set up seismographs all around the world. When an earthquake strikes, its seismic waves travel and are recorded at different locations. This helps the seismologists find the epicenter, or where the earthquake began. How? P-waves travel faster than S-waves, so they reach a seismograph first. Seismologists calculate the time difference between when the two waves arrive. This tells them how far away the epicenter is from the location of the seismograph.

Next, seismologists draw a circle on a map. The seismograph's location is in the middle of the circle. The length from the circle's center to its edge is equal to how far away the earthquake occurred. The epicenter lies somewhere within that circle. To figure out where, seismologists get data from two other seismographs. They draw circles around the location of each one on the map. The point where the three circles meet is the earthquake's epicenter.

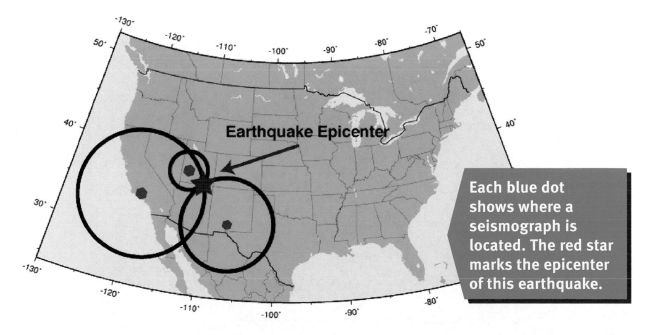

Earthquake Epicenter

Each blue dot shows where a seismograph is located. The red star marks the epicenter of this earthquake.

Measuring Earthquakes

Seismologists also measure an earthquake's size, or **magnitude**. They use the moment magnitude scale. It measures all of the energy released during an earthquake. It classifies earthquakes from minor, magnitude 3.0 to 3.9, to great, magnitude 8.0 or more. Each time there is an increase of a whole number, the ground shakes 10 times more. This means a magnitude 6.0 quake is 10 times stronger than one measuring 5.0.

A village in Nepal is destroyed after a 7.8 moment magnitude earthquake shook the country in April 2015.

Earthquakes that happen in Mexico City cause major damage. The city is built on an ancient lake bed, so the soil is loose.

Earthquakes are also measured by intensity, or how much shaking they cause. The intensity of a single earthquake can be very different from one place to another. The main things that affect intensity are the distance from the epicenter and the direction the seismic waves are traveling. What's in the ground matters, too. A house built on loose soil will shake a lot more than one built on solid rock.

Geologists study how earthquakes change landscapes over time.

Earthquake Geology

A geologist is another type of scientist who studies earthquakes. Geologists make maps of faults and the landforms around them. They dig in **fault zones** and study changes in the layers of rock and soil. They also measure faults and track how they move to find places where faults may be stuck or ready to break apart. By studying the history of faults, geologists can identify places where earthquakes are likely to occur.

Earthquake Myths

In ancient Greece, people believed earthquakes happened when Poseidon, god of the sea, got angry. We now know that isn't true. But myths about earthquakes are still around. For example, some people believe animals can sense when earthquakes are coming. There is no scientific proof of this. Others think big earthquakes only happen in the morning or on hot, dry days. But history shows that earthquakes can happen at any time and in all kinds of weather.

Poseidon is shown holding a trident. The myth says he struck his trident to the ground to cause earthquakes.

Do Earthquakes Only

Technically, yes. "Earth"quakes only happen on Earth. But quakes may happen in other places in our solar system. Discover a few of these places and how their quakes compare to what we experience on Earth.

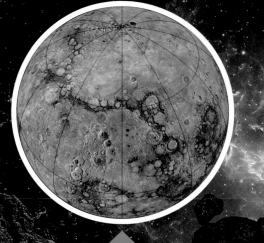

Mercury

Mercury's hot core has been cooling for a long time. As a result, the planet has been shrinking and cracking. This causes quakes. Scientists think this is still happening, meaning mercuryquakes likely rattle the planet's surface.

Venus

There are thousands of volcanoes on the surface of Venus. But do venusquakes shake its surface? None have ever been recorded, but scientists have new experiments in the works to find out.

Happen on Earth?

Neil Armstrong and Buzz Aldrin put a seismograph on the moon in 1969.

Mars
NASA's InSight lander touched down on Mars in November 2018. Since then, it has detected hundreds of rumbles deep beneath the planet's surface. Scientists think marsquakes are caused as the planet's core cools and its crust shrinks and cracks.

Earth's Moon
Moonquakes are common. They happen when a meteor strikes or when huge changes in temperature occur as sides of the moon go from day to night. The strongest moonquakes happen because the moon is cooling, shrinking, and cracking—just like Mercury and Mars.

Japan has about 1,500 earthquakes each year.

On March 11, 2011, the magnitude 9.0 Great Sendai Earthquake shook northeastern Japan.

Famous Earthquakes

People start to feel earthquakes at around magnitude 3.0. These minor quakes make the ground shake about as much as if a big truck passed by. Other earthquakes are so deadly and destructive that people continue to talk about them centuries later. Here are some of the most impactful earthquakes ever recorded.

Shaanxi Earthquake

The Shaanxi earthquake lasted just seconds. But when the magnitude 8.0 quake struck central China on January 23, 1556, it caused massive damage hundreds of miles from the epicenter. An area measuring 520 miles (840 kilometers) wide was destroyed. The quake leveled mountains and changed the path of rivers. Landslides swept away entire villages. The quake killed about 830,000 people and is believed to be the deadliest earthquake ever recorded.

Many people in Shaanxi lived in house caves carved into cliffs. They died when their homes collapsed.

About two million people were left homeless after the Chilean earthquake and tsunami in 1960.

The Great Chilean Earthquake

The most powerful earthquake ever recorded happened on May 22, 1960. A 621-mile-long (1,000 km) section of a fault snapped just off the southern coast of Chile. It triggered a magnitude 9.5 earthquake. The earthquake started a giant tsunami that devastated Chile's coastline before racing across the Pacific Ocean. It hit Hawaii, Japan, and then the Philippines.

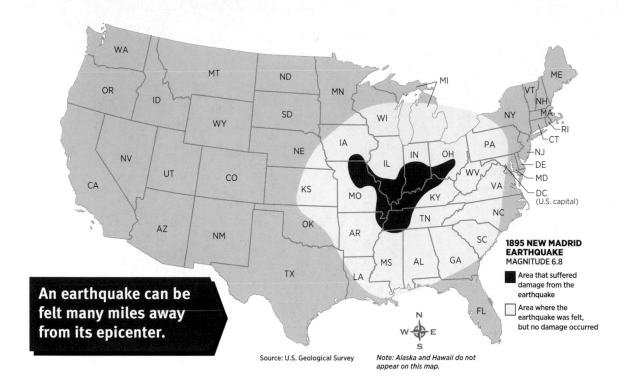

An earthquake can be felt many miles away from its epicenter.

1895 NEW MADRID EARTHQUAKE
MAGNITUDE 6.8

■ Area that suffered damage from the earthquake

□ Area where the earthquake was felt, but no damage occurred

Source: U.S. Geological Survey

Note: Alaska and Hawaii do not appear on this map.

New Madrid Earthquakes

During the winter of 1811–12, the New Madrid Seismic Zone in the central United States sprung to life. It is located in the middle of a tectonic plate. There were three major earthquakes in the mid-7 magnitude range and thousands of aftershocks. Then in 1895, another large earthquake struck the area. Its effects were felt across a large part of the eastern half of the United States.

San Andreas Fault

Perhaps the most famous earthquake of all—the "Big One"—is the one scientists fear will come sometime in the future. It is predicted to happen along the San Andreas Fault, an 800-mile-long (1,290 km) fault zone in California. Thousands of small earthquakes happen there each year. Big earthquakes occur there about every 200 years. Seismologists constantly watch the fault for signs that the next Big One is about to strike.

The next Big One could cause major damage. Many large cities such as Los Angeles (pictured) are near the San Andreas Fault.

San Francisco

CALIFORNIA

San Andreas Fault

Los Angeles

Great Alaska Earthquake

On March 27, 1964, one tectonic plate suddenly slipped beneath another in southeastern Alaska. This triggered a magnitude 9.2 earthquake that shook the ground for nearly five minutes. It was so strong that rivers and lakes splashed as far away as Texas and Louisiana. The earthquake created massive landslides and caused deadly tsunamis in the Pacific Ocean. It was the second largest earthquake ever recorded.

Timeline of Earthquake Discoveries

132 CE
Zhang Heng invents the seismoscope.

1850
Seismic waves are discovered.

1872
Geologists figure out that earthquakes occur along fault lines.

1897
P-waves, S-waves, and surface waves are identified.

San Francisco

San Andreas Fault

CALIFORNIA

Los Angeles

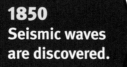

Indian Ocean Earthquake

A magnitude 9.1 earthquake occurred off the coast of the island of Sumatra, Indonesia, on December 26, 2004. The earthquake caused the ocean floor to suddenly rise, triggering a massive tsunami. Within 20 minutes, 100-foot (30 m) waves smashed onto the shore. The tsunami raced across the Indian Ocean. It hit South Africa eight hours after the earthquake occurred. This was one of the deadliest disasters in modern history, claiming nearly 230,000 lives.

1912
The idea that continents drift, which leads to the idea of tectonic plates, is introduced.

1935
The Richter magnitude scale is developed. It is the main method used to measure the strength of earthquakes until the 1970s.

1979
The moment magnitude scale is created. It replaces the use of the Richter magnitude scale and is the main method used today.

2020
NASA develops technology to monitor earthquakes from space.

You may only have 10 seconds to take cover once an earthquake starts.

An earthquake emergency kit should include everything you'd need to survive for at least three days.

Earthquake Safety

Earthquakes happen suddenly, so it's important to plan ahead to stay safe if one occurs. First, make your home as safe as possible. Bolt heavy furniture to the wall and put latches on cabinets. This will keep things from falling. Next, create an earthquake emergency kit with everything you'll need if someone is hurt or your home loses power. Then, plan an escape route and practice it with your family.

Staying Safe During an Earthquake

When an earthquake starts, don't panic. Instead, drop to the ground immediately. Cover your head and neck with your arms. If you're in bed, cover your head with a pillow. Stay put until the shaking stops. Keep away from windows and exterior walls. They're the first places to break during an earthquake. Avoid elevators. They may stop working. If you're outside, move away from buildings and other things that could hurt you.

One of the safest places to be during an earthquake is under a sturdy table.

Most injuries sustained during earthquakes happen when people try to move around.

Search and rescue dogs are trained to find people who are trapped after an earthquake.

Road to Recovery

After the shaking stops, stay alert. The danger may not be over yet. There could be aftershocks, landslides, or even tsunamis along the coast. If you're trapped, stay calm and call out for help. If you're not trapped, check yourself for injuries and get help if you need it. Help others if you can. Call your family to let them know you're okay if you're not home. But don't go home until you know it's safe.

Engineering a Safer Future

Today, technology helps keep people safe during earthquakes. Early warning systems send alerts to cell phones, which gives people extra time to find cover. New materials make it possible for bridges to bend during earthquakes instead of cracking and falling apart. This keeps people safe on the roads. Scientists are even testing high-tech buoys that can sense small movements on the ocean floor.

Parts added beneath this bridge absorb seismic waves. The bridge will now shake less during an earthquake.

This buoy located off the coast of Thailand detects movement in the ocean and sends warnings of possible tsunamis.

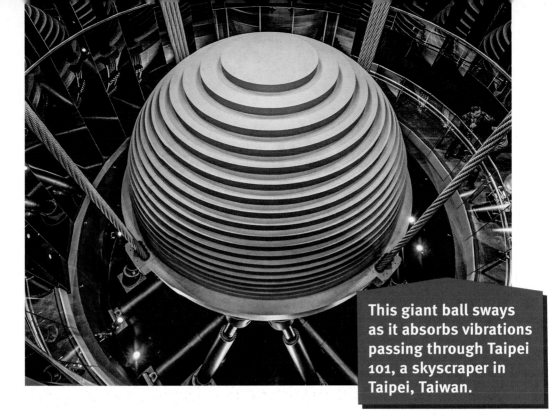

This giant ball sways as it absorbs vibrations passing through Taipei 101, a skyscraper in Taipei, Taiwan.

Some places that have lots of earthquakes also have many skyscrapers. Engineers have found ways to keep them from crumbling when the ground shakes. The buildings are built on thick rubber pads in the ground that absorb seismic waves. They also have specially designed parts that keep the walls from shaking too much. Experts continue to think of new ideas that will help keep people and our towns and cities safer well into the future.

Predicting Earthquake Risk

Earthquakes can cause a lot of damage. Knowing where they are most likely to occur helps people prepare. This map of the United States shows where earthquakes are expected to cause damage in the next 100 years. Study the map, and then answer the questions that follow.

Analyze It!

1. Which color shows areas that have the greatest chance of a damaging earthquake occurring?

2. How likely is it that a damaging earthquake will occur in these areas?

Chance of Damaging Earthquakes in the United States

Note: Alaska and Hawaii do not appear on this map.

Source: U.S. Geological Survey

Chance of damaging earthquake in the next 100 years

- **Very high** (More than 74%)
- **High** (36.1% to 74%)
- **Medium** (19.1% to 36%)
- **Low** (4% to 19%)
- **Very low** (Less than 4%)

3 Which state is more likely to have a damaging earthquake: Washington or Missouri?

4 Is the overall chance of a damaging earthquake greater on the East Coast, on the West Coast, or in the Midwest? Why do you think that is?

ANSWERS: 1. Red 2. More than 74% 3. Washington 4. The West Coast; The West Coast lies on tectonic plate borders. This is where most earthquakes occur.

Create an Earthquake-Proof Structure

The right design is an important part of creating earthquake-proof buildings. Do you have some good ideas? Here's a fun way to put them to the test.

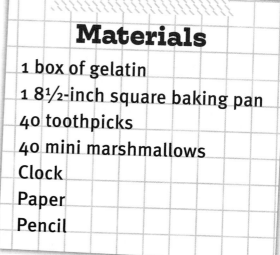

Materials

1 box of gelatin
1 8½-inch square baking pan
40 toothpicks
40 mini marshmallows
Clock
Paper
Pencil

Directions

1 Follow instructions on the package and prepare the gelatin in the baking pan. Let it set overnight.

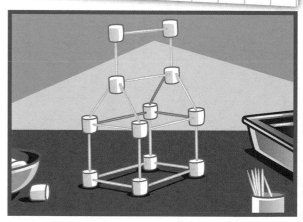

2 Design and build a structure using half of the toothpicks and mini marshmallows. It should be at least 6 inches (15 centimeters) tall.

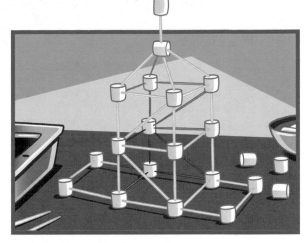

 3 Place the building on the gelatin base. Shake the pan for 10 seconds. Examine what happens to your building and record the results.

4 Use the remaining supplies to design and build a second structure. Challenge yourself to make it taller and stronger than the first.

5 Place building number two on the gelatin base. Shake the pan for 10 seconds. Examine what happens and then compare what you see with the results of your first trial.

Explain It!

Using what you learned in the book, can you explain what happened and why? If you need help, turn back to pages 38–39.

True Statistics

Percentage of earthquakes that occur along tectonic plate borders: 90

Average distance tectonic plates move along the San Andreas Fault each year: 2 inches (5 cm)

Number of earthquakes that occur each year: Millions

Magnitude of strongest earthquake ever recorded: 9.5 (Valdivia, Chile, in 1960)

Magnitude of strongest recorded moonquake: 5.5

Length of the longest-lasting earthquake ever recorded: About 10 minutes (Valdivia, Chile, in 1960)

Length of the Ring of Fire: About 24,000 miles (40,000 km)

Depth of most earthquakes: 50 miles (80 km) or less below Earth's surface

Cost of the 2011 earthquake in Japan—the most expensive earthquake ever: $232 billion

Did you find the truth?

 (T) Earthquakes happen along cracks in Earth's surface.

(F) Most earthquakes happen in an area surrounding the Atlantic Ocean.

Resources

Other books in this series:

You can also look at:

Furgang, Kathy. *Everything Volcanoes and Earthquakes*. Washington, DC: National Geographic Kids, 2013.

Hoobler, Dorothy, and Thomas Hoobler. *What Was the San Francisco Earthquake?* New York: Grosset & Dunlap, 2016.

Perish, Patrick. *Survive an Earthquake*. New York: Children's Press, 2017.

Van Rose, Susanna. *Volcanoes & Earthquakes*. New York: DK Children, 2014.

Woolf, Alex. *The Science of Natural Disasters: The Devastating Truth About Volcanoes, Earthquakes, and Tsunamis*. New York: Children's Press, 2018.

Glossary

earthquake (URTH-kwayk) a sudden, violent shaking of the earth that may damage buildings and cause injuries

epicenter (EP-i-sen-tur) the area directly above where an earthquake occurs. Often, the people who live at or near the epicenter are in the greatest danger during an earthquake.

fault (fawlt) a large break in Earth's surface that can cause an earthquake

fault zones (fawlt zohnz) areas with many faults

magnitude (MAG-ni-tood) the size of an earthquake

mass (mas) the amount of physical matter that an object contains

seismic waves (SIZE-mik wayvz) waves that carry energy released by an earthquake

seismographs (SIZE-muh-grafs) instruments that detect earthquakes and measure their power

seismologists (size-MAH-luh-jists) scientists who study seismic waves

tectonic plate boundaries (tek-TAH-nik playt BOWN-dur-eez) edges where tectonic plates meet

tectonic plates (tek-TAH-nik playts) huge sections of Earth's crust and topmost mantle layer that move very slowly

tsunamis (tsu-NAH-meez) fast-moving and dangerous waves caused by underwater earthquakes or volcanoes

Index

Page numbers in **bold** indicate illustrations.

About the Author

Libby Romero was a journalist and teacher before becoming an author. She studied agricultural journalism at the University of Missouri-Columbia (B.S. and B.J.) and received her M.Ed. from Marymount University in Arlington, Virginia. As a child, she read nearly every nonfiction book in her school's library. Now she's added dozens of new books to the shelves. She lives in Virginia with her husband and two sons.